Chasing the Rain

My Treasure Hunt for the World's Most Beautiful Mushrooms

Taylor F. Lockwood

Published by:
Taylor F. Lockwood
P. O. Box 1412
Mendocino
California 95460
U.S.A.

First edition, first printing
For ordering information please write to the above address or visit:
www.KingdomofFungi.com

All photography by Taylor F. Lockwood unless otherwise noted
Design: Taylor F. Lockwood
Proofreader: Annette Jarvie
Indexer: Medea Minnich
Map reproductions from *Survey Atlas of the World*, J.G. Bartholomew, 1922
Mushroom on page 2, *Cystolepiota* sp.

Printed in China
ISBN: 978-0-9709449-2-4

Nature/Travel/Photography

Michigan pond

Contents

About the Photos

It must be the explorer in me—I love the unknown. The Kingdom of Fungi has many unknowns and that keeps the mycologists and mushroom photographers very busy. This book features as many new and unidentified mushrooms as I can reasonably fit into it. When I had a choice between ones that were already named, versus the ones that are unidentified and of equal aesthetic appeal, I often chose the latter. As I was writing this book, I was notified that one of the mushrooms in the New Zealand chapter (*Dermocybe austrovenata*, page 34) had not been previously recorded there.

A few images are included here from my first book, *Treasures from the Kingdom of Fungi,* when they are the focus of a story or have special appeal. These photos are marked with (TKF) in the captions.

About the People

In this book, I touch upon several facets of mushrooming and mycology. But, there is one social aspect that deserves special attention. A unique relationship exists between many amateur mushroom hunters and the professional mycologists. It is a rare symbiosis in which the amateurs need the professionals for their scientific knowledge and the professionals need the amateurs to help collect and record new material for study.

For those who are just discovering this special kingdom, you will find a fascinating blend of scientific, medicinal, social, spiritual, and gastronomic worlds. Above all, you'll find one more reason to love our beautiful and bountiful Earth!

Dedication

This book is dedicated to the many people who have provided me with information, encouragement, mushroom identifications, and a place to lay my head as I pursued my mycological treasure hunts.

Agaricus augustus under discarded rug, California

Introduction

In 1993, after finishing a presentation to a group on the east coast, I had an epiphany. I realized that through my photography, I was in a special position to help raise awareness of and appreciation for mushrooms and other fungi. I was single, self-employed, motivated, and I really believed *mushrooms needed me.*

Within a couple of years, I discovered computers, and I began e-mailing and exchanging photos with mushroomers all over the world. I traveled to Australia and New Zealand, the Amazon, and many other countries, all for the love of fungi. What started as a hobby had become a passion quest to find the world's most beautiful mushrooms.

I've had plenty of hits and some near misses along the way. Although it's all influenced by rainfall, the number of hits I get is also a matter of persistence. I have had many instances of getting great shots on the last day, in the last hour, or on the way to the airport. This comes from believing that there is always something out there, something that you would really like to find, but didn't. This can be baffling to your hosts, who might want to show you their new civic center on a day that you could be hunting mushrooms.

I published my first book, *Treasures from the Kingdom of Fungi,* as a photo essay in 2001. Although I had been writing stories about my travels for years before then, I opted not to include them at that time. I was sure I would have another opportunity to share my adventures.

Chasing the Rain is a collection of my favorite mushroom photographs since the *Treasures* book. It also includes photos of people, travel stories, letters, field notes, and anecdotes about mushrooms and mushrooming. And, more importantly, it is one man's observation of how the culture of mushrooms connects people all over the world.

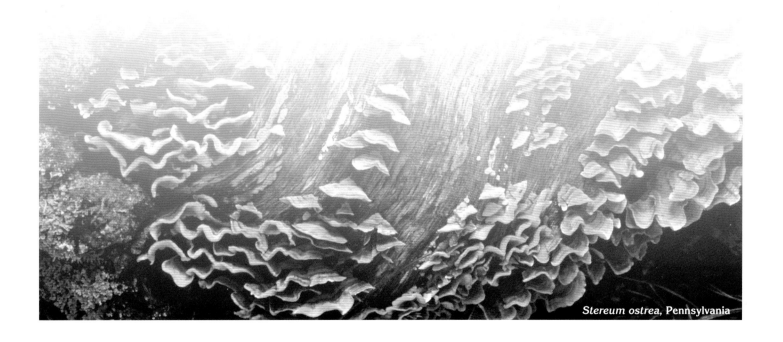

Stereum ostrea, Pennsylvania

Lamington National Park, Queensland, Australia

Chasing the Rain

Discovery

Mendocino, California
December 1984

After seven years of heat, smog, and rock-and-roll, I left Los Angeles for greener surroundings and cleaner air. I wanted to be north of San Francisco but still in California, so I meandered up and down the coast until I happened upon the sleepy little artist town of Mendocino. Sensing that this was a good place to stay and get my bearings, I moved into a secluded cabin surrounded by trees and a view of the Pacific Ocean.

It was an unusually warm, wet winter. Within a week, I was so impressed by the beautiful mushrooms in the surrounding woods, that I wanted to take their portraits. I went to the local camera store and bought a camera, flash, macro lens, and film—with mushrooms on my mind.

Taylor Lockwood, Mendocino, California, 1984

Montgomery Woods, Mendocino, California

Though my first photos were not very impressive, I had years of art in my life and a sense of what I wanted to accomplish. After a lot of experimentation with camera, flash, reflectors, and many rolls of film, I started seeing some acceptable results. After about nine months of continuous mushroom hunting and photography, I attended a local photographers' group meeting. I learned that if your goal was to publish your work, slide film was the medium of choice. By the time I shot my first roll of slide film, I had quite a bit of experience behind me. So when I opened my first box of processed slides, I was amazed. The images were beautiful! Although beauty is relative and my standards have changed and risen over time, I still have some images in my catalog from that first roll.

Young *Gomphus floccosus* from the first roll of slides

In 1985, I started meeting other people who were into mushrooms. In December of that year, I attended the San Francisco Fungus Fair at the Hall of Flowers in Golden Gate Park. People were very friendly and touched by my newfound passion and the prints that fruited from it. There were many introductions, but one of the most memorable was to the president of the Los Angeles Mycological Society (LAMS), Greg Wright. Not considering that my words were closer to aspiration than to reality, I told him I had a slide show of mushroom photographs set to music. He seemed mildly interested and went on his way, as I did mine.

About three weeks later, I got a letter from Greg saying that he had talked it over with the organizing council for the LAMS mushroom fair, and they were inviting me as a special guest to present my show. Oh my god! I had no show! However, I realized this was a special opportunity, so I decided to give it my best shot.

I took a reel-to-reel tape recorder to the house of some friends who had a good selection of baroque and classical music. Armed with recording skills I learned in Hollywood,

Stropharia ambigua with show logo

I edited, cut, and spliced over the next several days until I produced something I was happy with.

However, at that point, I hadn't yet given a mushroom show, and I was very nervous. I spent the remainder of the week shuffling slides into the program I called "The Hidden Forest." Nervous or not, I presented the show for the first time at the 1986 LAMS Mushroom Fair and got a standing ovation for my efforts. The spores of passion had germinated!

In time, I changed the name of the program to "Treasures from the Kingdom of Fungi." Over the next fifteen years, I showed it hundreds of times in America and other parts of the world.

From the "Treasures" slide show

Elements of Style

When I started out, I knew I wanted to use electronic flash to get the proper colors of the mushrooms on film. Forest canopies usually filter out red and yellow light, so uncorrected photography using natural light often produces a blue-gray cast to the images.

Hygrocybe coccineus

Because of the terrain in this area (steep hillsides with lots of fallen trees), I could just as easily shoot up at a mushroom as shoot down. This gave me what has become an important element, almost a signature of my style—the gill shot. And, through the use of light above and camera below methods, I became fascinated by and endeared to the translucence of the mushrooms. The result was more dramatic, high contrast images.

Pleurocybella porrigens

The Jiffypop Connection

I wasn't very happy with the harsh shadows in some of my photographs. I needed something that softened the flash yet, unlike a photo umbrella, would direct the light right to the small scenes I was photographing. I needed a lightweight, portable, diffusing reflector which I could attach to my flash unit easily—one that could be repaired or replaced easily, as well. It became apparent to me that I would have to make the equipment I wanted.

After trying various pans, pie tins, and other reflective items, I found the perfect light redirector, an empty Jiffypop pan. It came with a built-in handle, which I could bend to fit my flash unit. With tape or rubber bands, it would stay in place as long as I needed it.

This generally worked very well, as long as the subject was not highly

Mycena abramsii

reflective. If it was, the results could be unpredictable, unless I was very conscious of the reflections on the mushroom I was photographing. The Jiffypop system lasted for a few years, until I refined the flash unit even more.

By the time I went to Australia in 1995, I had taken apart and rewired my main flash incorporating a parabolic reflector which allowed me to direct the light straight down (like softened, natural sunlight) or any other direction I chose. This design, with the addition of other flash heads, remains the heart of my lighting equipment to this day.

As time went on though, I became increasingly interested in having more of the surroundings in my photos while still featuring the subjects and their gills in the light of my flashes. This is accomplished using a tripod (I use a modified Benbo Trekker) and the addition of natural light.

As this book is roughly chronological, you will see the evolution of my technique, from the dramatic to the more subtle and inclusive, as you go through the chapters.

Cortinarius vanduzerensis

Working a log in Queensland, Australia (mushroom photo pg. 25)

Panus conchatus, California

Russula aff. *azurea*, California

Hypomyces chrysospermum, California

Ramaria araiospora, California

Hygrocybe flavescens, California

Agaricus augustus, California

Chasing the Rain

Aleuria aurantia, California

Amanita gemmata, California

Hygrocybe sp., California

Clitocybe nebularis, California

Crepidotus sp., California

Hygrocybe laeta, California

Hohenbuehelia mastrucata, California

Russula rosacea, California

Chasing the Rain

Xeromphalina campanella, California

Bolbitius vitellinus, California

Arcangeliella sp., California

Ardean Watts, Utah

Spathularia velutipes, North Carolina

Stropharia kaufmanii, Oregon

Phyllotopsis nidulans, Wisconsin

18

Chasing the Rain

Branching Out

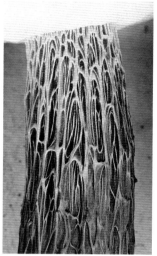

Boletus sp., Idaho

Over the next few years, I expanded my hunting range to include all of California and the West Coast, the Rockies, and then the rest of the country. I had a great time meeting the wide range of interesting people who are into mushrooms (like Ardean Watts, facing page). As I went, I asked a lot of questions and became aware of the vast knowledge that many of them possess.

One thing I found especially interesting is that regionality is very important, not only to identification, but to the likelihood of finding rare or unusual species. I've been very lucky to have seen so many varieties of mushrooms on my travels. However, those who are locals always have the advantage of being there when the mushrooms appear. No matter where you live or travel, there is always the potential of finding something that is unusual, rare, or just shouldn't be there.

For example, the South and the East Coast of the U.S. are known for having many Boletes with heavily reticulate stems. At one foray in Priest Lake, Idaho, I found one that looked like it came from thousands of miles away! Another time, I offered some images to a Seattle group for their yearly poster. After reviewing the images, a local mycologist said that one of the species was only known from the Midwest and farther east. As my image catalog is strictly chronological, I determined that the species in question, *Microglossum rufum*, was taken before I ever left the west coast!

Revelations about mushrooming and mycology are continuous and frequent. They feed the passion of the mushroom world. No one mycologist knows them all, and even amateurs find mushrooms that were previously unknown.

Microglossum rufum,
Washington

Russia, Finland, & Sweden

The Trans-Siberian Express
July 1989

In 1987, I was invited to attend a Key Council meeting in the Oregon Cascades of about twenty mycologists and other mushroomers. At the meeting, there was an adventurer and entrepreneur from Seattle named Dennis Bowman. As I had grown up in Seattle, I developed an easy rapport with him. At one point Dennis pulled me aside and said he was planning a mushroom foray to Russia with the main destination being Siberia. Without hesitation I said, "Denny, I'm in." It would be the first of many foreign mushroom adventures for me.

So in July 1989, a group of a dozen or so mushroomers from all over the United States met in Seattle, flew over the pole, and landed in Moscow. After a few days there, we spent fifty-two hours on the trans-Siberian express to Novosibirsk. Upon arriving at five o'clock in the morning, we were greeted by our hosts with the customary Russian welcome of bread and salt. By the next day, we had met a wonderful group of people who shared our interest in mushrooms, peace, and parties!

Unfortunately for my mushroom photography, it was very dry. But we had a great time anyway. Our hosts treated us to a *shashlik* (a Tartar-style cook-out), and we did a lot of exploring in the villages around the area.

I had been asked to present my "Treasures from the Kingdom of Fungi" slide show. Their audio-visual equipment was minimal, but I made do with a hand-operated slide projector and a very small cassette player. It all worked well, and the Russians were very appreciative. I realized then that our mutual interest in mushrooms

St. Basil's Cathedral, Moscow

Train locomotive emblem

was a powerful force that superseded the barriers of language and culture.

Denny had told us this would be an adventure, and he was right. Up until the time we flew into Leningrad on the return trip, none of his contacts there had heard of the hotel we were supposed to be staying in! As it turned out, it was a *boat*, a fancy Finnish boat, on the Neva River in the middle of the city. Denny managed to get us there before dark, and we slept well that night.

The show must go on!

Because it had rained there recently, Leningrad turned out to be my best chance to find mushrooms to photograph. Everyone else in the group wanted to see the Summer Palace, so Denny and some Russian friends took me out to a rural area and dropped me off in the woods. I got some good shots, and though I knew no Russian, I walked and mimed and pointed until I got back to the city. As I made my way back, I saw older Russian women carrying baskets with mushrooms that must have had radioactive traces from Chernobyl. For that matter, after crawling through the forest, maybe I did too!

After leaving Russia, I had stopovers with forays and shows in both Finland and Sweden. There, as well as in Russia, it was touching to see the roots of our appreciation for mushrooms that are still seen in ethnic communities in America.

Although the trip was not a bonanza for finding great quantities of mushrooms to photograph, I did find a few beautiful ones. One of the best, and new to me at the time, was a *Stropharia aeruginosa* from Finland (pg. 23).

Mushroom market

Pickled mushrooms on the Trans-Siberian Express

Mushroom toothbrush holder

Mushrooms at a Novosibirsk market

Russian plate featuring *Amanita muscaria*

Leccinum sp., Finland (TKF)

Russula aff. fragilis, Russia

Laccaria laccata, Russia

Lycoperdon perlatum, Russia (TKF)

Chasing the Rain

Stropharia aeruginosa, Finland (TKF)

Australia

New South Wales
May 1995

My first trip to Australia was also my first trip to the southern hemisphere. I didn't know what to expect other than the mushrooms were supposed to be "different" there. There are many mushrooms down under that are recognizable to topsiders, but there are also many odd, unique, and wonderful gems. Even after four photographic tours, there is a lot left for me to discover.

After a few letters to my contact there, Dr. Anthony (Tony) Young, I concluded that I should stick to the east coast and stay tuned to the weather reports. Australia's main mushroom season coincides with our spring, conveniently the same time my hayfever kicks in back home. I looked forward to missing that!

When I arrived, it was sunny, warm, and dry—like Southern California minus the smog. The people were friendly, and I felt that mushrooms or not, Australia was a great place to visit. After a day of renting a car and getting my bearings, I headed north out of Sydney to the next impressive sight, billions of eucalyptus trees.

Finding the rain to chase

I was a little concerned at first because it was hot and dry, and I had come for mushrooms. I soon learned from the locals that above these dry eucalyptus forests are many ancient hilltop rainforests. Coming from the

Lamington National Park, Queensland

Chasing the Rain

northwest U.S. where it is wet on the bottom and snowy on the top, it took some getting used to. But, I am happy with whatever works so, "get yer gear, mate!"

As I headed along the coast north of Sydney, there were many expansive public areas in which to hunt. I immediately found a few genera that I knew like *Coprinus*, *Lepiota*, and *Pholiota*, and many that I didn't. One of the oddest of them was something that no one to date has identified. I call it the "brown mystery." It could be a fungus, an animal, an insect's nest, or some combination.

Several days later, I made it up to Tony's place in Queensland, saw his mycological lab, and sampled his fine homemade beer. The next day he took me to a magical rainforest on top of the Bunya Mountains. The trees seemed to be out of the dinosaur era with many vines hanging from them. There was no shortage of mushrooms, and I kept very busy photographing them. After leaving Tony's the next day I went to Lamington National Park. There I found many different species including clumps of small but bright, blue mushrooms later identified as *Mycena interrupta*.

After a few days of photography, recording birdsongs, and spending nights sleeping in my car, I followed Tony's suggestion to head south—way south—to Tasmania.

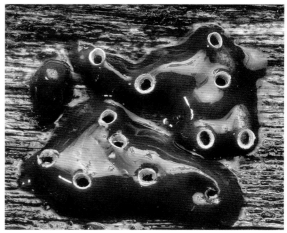
Unidentified

Dr. Anthony Young

Pholiota sp.

Mycena interrupta

Tasmania, Log notes May 1995

I am now in southwestern Tasmania, and Tony was right. There are mushrooms everywhere. Out on the road to Strathgordon, I must have seen thousands of about fifty or sixty different species. I found a *Pleurotus* with a very dark cap, and a flush of Boletes with red caps, lemon yellow pores, and white dots on their stipes. One of them was stunning! My guidebook calls them *Boletellus obscurecoccineus*.

Pleurotus purpureo-olivaceus

Boletellus obscurecoccineus (TKF)

Today I returned to a great spot called "Growling Swallet." It's a place where a small river disappears into a limestone cave only to reappear many miles away. It is a stunning sight, and growl it does.

The trail to it has lots of mushrooms. I went there in the rain two days ago, but my equipment got wet, so I returned to my room to dry it off. Today, however, I found several viscid, blue *Cortinarius rotundisporus* as well as some dark green *Hygrocybes* they call *Gliophorus* here. The best news of the day, no leeches!

I'm doing well driving on the left side of the road, but I keep getting in on the wrong side of the car!

Growling Swallet

Cortinarius rotundisporus

Gliophorus sp. (*Hygrocybe* sp.)

Mt Field, Tasmania
May 1995

It was late fall with touches of frost on the ground. I had been out in the woods all day, and it was getting too dark to hunt mushrooms, so I headed back toward my lonely little hostel. I had been the only guest the previous night, so I expected the same for that evening. But, when I drove in towards the building, there was a big, old, station wagon with a curly-headed guy coming out of it. After a few light exchanges about placement of cars, he said he was from America, and he had come to hunt fungi. "Wow," I thought to myself, "I'm at the end of the Earth, and I find someone else who has come here for mushrooms!"

He had brought his wife and three kids, making the place a lot more lively and welcoming. As I came in with my gear, I said, "I think I know you," and handed him my card, which read "Taylor F. Lockwood – Mushroom Photographer." As he blinked in surprise, he introduced himself as Dr. Rytas Vilgalys, professor of mycology at Duke University. I said I remembered him from the 1994 NAMA (North American Mycological Association) foray in Montreat, North Carolina.

We had the whole place to ourselves. Rytas had set up a mini-lab in the living room, and we had Cascade Dark Beer from the pub across the street. Over talk of *Amanitas* and accordians (we both play), we started a friendship that would help me in my future travels.

These mounds average about 5 ft. high

Red termite mounds from red earth

The spines mean you're getting close!

Podaxis beringamensis revealing black spore mass

Podaxis beringamensis can grow to be 3 ft. high

Queensland
March 2004

O ne of the oddest and most interesting forays I've ever had was up in the Atherton tablelands of Queensland. I had been staying at the Cape Tribulation Tropical Research Station while looking for stinkhorns and other fungi. A suggestion by the director, Dr. Hugh Spencer, sent me inland north of the town of Mt. Malloy. There I might see, if I were lucky, some termite mound fungi.

Many species of termites have a symbiotic relationship with fungi. They cultivate the mycelium as food in a garden deep in the mound. If and when the termites abandon the mound, the mushrooms start fruiting out of the mycelial garden, up through the mound, and then out the top.

Hunting for these entails checking a lot of termite mounds at a time when the fungi might be fruiting. You drive down the road very slowly, watching constantly to make sure you aren't rear-ended. You might have to scan over thousands of mounds before you see anything, especially when you're not exactly sure what you're looking for!

After a day or so, I managed to find a few "spines," the leftover backbone of each fruit body. Then, as my eyes and mind got tuned into what I was looking for, I found one, then two, and more. After I collected a specimen, Dr. Tom May from the Royal Botanic Gardens in Melbourne confirmed their identity as *Podaxis beringamensis*.

A few days and thousands of termite mounds later, I returned to the coast. The weather report said that Southern Queensland just had thirteen inches of rain. The chase was on, and I headed for the airport.

Boletellus ananas

Chasing the Rain

Deflexula subsimplex

Lentinus tuberregium

Podoserpula pusio

Geastrum minimum

Coprinus ephemerus

Pluteus atromarginatus

Mycena nargan

Hygrocybe graminicolor

Entoloma virescens

Chasing the Rain

Craterellus aff. *aureus*

Ramaria sp.

Fistulinella mollis

Armillaria luteobubalina

Mycena viscidocruenta

New Zealand

Okuru
May 2002

I visited the North Island of New Zealand in 1995 and the South Island in 2002. The forest scenery there is some of the best I have seen. There were lichens everywhere, epiphytes dripping from the trees, and mushrooms waiting to be discovered. With their ancient tree ferns and beech trees, it is magic!

I had often hoped to get to the New Zealand yearly foray, and on my second trip, I finally made it. In attendance were professional and amateur mycologists collecting and studying some of the most wonderfully weird and interesting fungi on Earth.

Photography was good, and some of the mushrooms were spectacular. After the foray I headed south to the fiordland town of Te Anau and found nearby forest floors covered with mushrooms.

Above and below: *Weraroa virescens* (TKF)

South Island, West Coast

One of the groups that has fascinated me since I first visited New Zealand is the stalked, gastroid fungi. They are commonly called "pouch fungi," and unlike mushrooms with caps and gills, their caps remain closed with the spore mass inside. Apparently, their spore distribution is facilitated by insects and ground-dwelling birds. Consequently, they are often brightly colored and make great photo subjects. Pictured on page thirty-two is *Weraroa virescens,* and on this page, some others of this group.

Thaxterogaster porphyreum

Unidentified

Weraroa erythrocephala (lower right) lost in the berries

On my first visit in 1995, I was amazed to see what looked like a discarded red bell pepper (known as *capsicum* down there) on the forest floor. It wasn't a vegetable, though. It was a fungus called *Paurocotylis pila,* and ironically when I cut it open, it looked like the inside of a red bell pepper! On my 2002 trip, I found the "blue potato fungus" or *Gautieria novaezelandiae,* and another earthball with incredibly beautiful violet color called *Gallacea scleroderma.* A little more recognizable was a *Calostoma rodwayi.* We have another related species, *Calostoma cinnabarina,* on the east coast of North America.

Paurocotylis pila (TKF)

Gautieria novaezelandiae

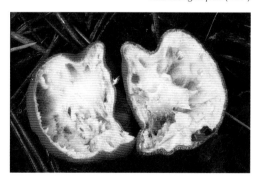
Paurocotylis pila, section

Gallacea scleroderma

Calostoma rodwayi

Cymatoderma elegans

Thaxterogaster porphyreum

Dermocybe austrovenata

Unidentified

Chasing the Rain

Stropharia aurantiaca

Armillaria sp.

Austroboletus niveus

Gliophorus viridis

¿Quien es El Niño?
March 1997

Like all good traveling mushroom photographers, I did my homework. I checked the weather for Chile every few days, checked the latitudes I would be visiting, got my maps, and researched the historical rainfall reports. I planned on being in Chile in March and April which, considering hemisphere and latitudes, should have about the same weather as our September and October on the west coast.

It was just about that time that meteorologists were coalescing their theories about the temperature of the southern Pacific Ocean, and its effect on the weather. The phenomenon that would throw me for a loop we now know as El Niño.

"No, Señor, mucha lluvia en enero" (It rained like crazy in January). Oh boy. While I was a bit dissappointed, I decided to make the best of it. I would enjoy the good weather, and headed south just in case it might rain there. The bad news was that I never saw a drop.

The good news was that I spent some easy time photographing wooden doors and painted boats in the

Volcan Osorno

Chasing the Rain

Puertas de Puerto Montt

Glacier near Chaitén

Mycena sp. (TKF)

southern port town of Puerto Montt. I also studied Spanish with a tutor there. The best news is that, El Niño or not, I still found mushrooms. Three of my mushroom photos from Chile rated high enough to be included in my first book, *Treasures from the Kingdom of Fungi.*

One of those (left), I found on a trek to a glacier south of Chaitén. Another, *Campanella aeruginea* (right), I found up in the foothills of the Andes. The third, a *Mycena* (upper right), has been a perennial favorite because of its minute size as shown next to a pencil.

I had made the best of an El Niño year. Now I was ready for the second half of my trip—the Peruvian Amazon.

Unidentified (also on pg. 38, lower left) (TKF)

Campanella aeruginea (TKF)

Chonchi, Isla de Chiloé

Mycena sp.

Unidentified

Unidentified

Lycoperdon sp.

Chasing the Rain

Pholiota sp.

Flammulina sp.

Unidentified

Psilocybe sp.

The Amazon

Down the Amazon
Peru
May 1997

After a relatively painless early morning stopover at the Lima airport, I caught my flight to Iquitos at 5:50 a.m. and arrived at about 8 a.m. My hosts at Project Amazonas had sent Fernando Rios to meet me. He waded through a slurry of taxi drivers and found me by holding a card bearing my name.

Mushroom hunting on the Rio Aroso

On the way through town, Fernando had the motorcar driver pull off to the side of the street next to an open-air restaurant. A big man with white hair and mustache stepped up to the car, stuck out his hand and with a friendly smile said, "Welcome to Iquitos!" Realizing that I hadn't met him before, Fernando offered, "Albert, Taylor, Taylor, Albert. "

Albert Slugocki was the founder of Project Amazonas (a U.S.-Peruvian nonprofit), and he had flown down

from Florida to check on its progress. It was a pleasant and unexpected surprise to meet him. Then we were off to the Hostal La Pascana to unload my gear, clean up, and relax a bit.

Soon after we got there Pedro arrived. I hired him not only as an interpreter but as an extra set of eyes. I would be concentrating on my photography out in the bush and not watching whatever might be crawling around, under, or on me while I was preoccupied. Both Fernando and Pedro seemed very anxious to make things as easy and comfortable as possible.

We arranged to meet in the morning to catch the pamacari down the river. After hearing many reports about thievery in Peru, I was bristling on guard as we came closer to the crowded market and launch where we would catch our boat. I was determined not to lose the equipment and supplies I had been carrying through Chile for the last two months. Pedro said that Fernando was unusually late, as our boat was to leave in ten minutes. So, for the third time he went walking through the market to where the boat was, and back. But still, no Fernando.

By this time, there were several sets of kids and young men hanging around near me. There were enough of them to make me feel uncomfortable about the well being of my suitcase, my camera gear, a bag full of batteries, and a bag of beer.

Then as I scanned the crowd for either Fernando or Pedro, I turned my head just in time to see the bag of beer being picked up and taken on its way to someone else's party. I yelled, lunged, and grabbed it back from the teenager who ambled away unsuccessfully. That maneuver was clearly a ploy to get me away from the more valuable things I had. Fortunately, it didn't work.

Pamacari heading upriver

Then one after the other Pedro and Fernando showed up, grabbed my suitcase and gear, and we were off through the crowded market. Now evermore bristling with justified paranoia, I was happy at least that we weren't hanging around and ready to be eaten alive by the *ratones* (street mice).

Then Fernando, after missing the action from a few minutes before, handed my equipment case to a kid to take to the boat. As he started heading out of sight, I took after him like a shot. After a long ten seconds, I caught up to him as he was dutifully heading towards the boat we were supposed to take.

After feeling comfortable for a minute or two, it was back to high alert when we were told to leave the gear on top of the low, sheet metal roof and get below. The boat was still docked and anything on top was only one step away from boats on either side and one step away from being history. To save on port taxes or a visit from the Peruvian police, we were supposed to look like a cargo boat. So, as we pulled out, I did my duty and went below.

Pamacari, an Amazon river bus

There were twenty to thirty people camped in the hold for the trip down the river with their hammocks strung up, their piglets tied up, and whatever supplies they had purchased in Iquitos. When we were safely out of sight of the police, I went back up and sat next to my gear for the eleven-hour ride.

We continued down the river, and the passengers, with their cargo, peeled off as we stopped at their thatched-roof houses or connections to them. It was getting dark when Fernando announced we were fifteen minutes away. Away from what I wasn't sure. We were fifteen minutes away from Yanashi, a village of thatched houses where the Yanashi River feeds into the Amazon. After docking, more people left with their supplies including blocks of ice, bags of rice, chickens, and piglets.

Thatched housing along the river

This was the pamacari's last stop of the day. Fernando's son, Segundo, was there to meet us with the Project Amazonas' swamp boat. It felt good to meet him and get my things off the pamacari. However, as I was getting ready for the hour-and-a-half ride through the swamp to the preserve, Fernando said there was some sort of problem. Pedro and I should stay in the village while Fernando and his son took care of some "business." Before I had a chance to think, they had launched and sped up the Yanashi River in the night with all my gear, leaving Pedro and I doubly in the dark.

Fernando had suggested that we take a walk while they tended to their "business," and they would return in an hour. Because there was no one to explain why this was all happening the way it was, we took a walk. The river had crested from the recent rains, so we walked for as long as we could until part of the walkway was under river water. We returned and as we waited, one hour turned to two hours, and I was beginning to feel very uncomfortable. Here I was, in the middle of nowhere, walking with a near stranger of dubious motivation. And, I was totally separated from my equipment, supplies, plane tickets, and plans—things that I had been so carefully guarding.

Fortunately, for fifteen or twenty minutes, the town television kept me from eating myself alive with worry. About twenty-five people, including Pedro and I, had our eyes glued to a flickering television that sat outside near the walkway for anyone to see. After we got our fill of that, we went back to the pamacari, and I had a good chance to stew over how I had gotten myself into this mess.

I hadn't thoroughly checked out the company that arranged this. I imagined, as Pedro and I were stuck on this strip of concrete, that Fernando and his son were probably stuffing who knows what kind of contraband items in the lining of my luggage, so I could be their stooge to carry it into the States. I envisioned what I would say to the customs officials if and when they found it. If it happened in the States, it would be a big problem. If it happened in Peru, it would be all over. And even if they just wanted my traveler's checks, plane tickets, and equipment, Pedro was sure to just disappear somewhere in Yanashi and leave me to face the group of young men that were collecting nearby in the dark.

I was just asking Pedro for the third hopeless time what was going on here, when Fernando and his son finally appeared with the boat. After some vague conversation between Fernando and Pedro, the "business" came out: the cook they scheduled couldn't show up until tomorrow, and they were running around looking for someone to cook dinner tonight! After I assured them I didn't care who cooked dinner, we headed off into the night toward the camp

The balsa

via a shortcut through the swamp. With Fernando guiding in front and his son deftly steering the motor in back, they took me out of my gringo hell into riverboat heaven, speeding through tight turns and ducking trees and vines by moonlight.

In an hour and a half we arrived at the *balsa*, their floating base camp with screened-in bedrooms, kitchen, showers, and workshop. As we made the loop to the dock, we were greeted by smiling faces. In an hour, we had dinner (cooked by Fernando) as we talked about several areas in which to hunt mushrooms. In another hour we were all sound asleep.

Chasing the Rain

Cookeina tricholoma

Xylaria sp.

Unidentified

Marasmius sp.

The Amazon   43

Lentinus aff. *concavus*

Coprinus sp.

Unidentified

Unidentified

Cordyceps sp.

Lentinus bertieri

Pleurotus sp.

Hygrocybe sp.

Southeast Asia
Thailand, Malaysia, & Southern China

The Taman Negara Forest
June 1998

I f the gecko on the wall was any indication, I had made it. I had just arrived from the U.S. on my first trip to Thailand, and was getting my bearings and orientation at a friend's house in Phuket. As I was recovering from two days of hard traveling and subsequent jet lag, I read an article about the Taman Negara forest in West Malaysia, just south of Thailand.

Within a couple of days, I was in Malaysia and on a train passing through rice fields, palm plantations, and beautiful jungle vegetation. After a brief stopover in the village of Kuala Lipis, a three-hour boat ride up the Jelai River took me deep into the Taman Negara forest to a small outpost. There were primitive open-air restaurants floating on the river and small, one-room cabins to camp in above the riverbank. It was thrilling to be so remote but have everything I needed. I went to sleep thinking about hunting mushrooms in the morning.

The next day, I found many mushrooms that I had never seen before, several of which were stunning. One had heavy violet flocculence covering the cap and another had magnificent blue gills.

After a few more days of fruitful mushroom hunting and photography, I took the boat back down the river, the train back to Thailand, and another train north to Chiang Mai.

Cystolepiota sp. (TKF)

Entoloma sp. (TKF)

Steamy haze near Bangkok

Chiang Mai
July 1998

After inquiring about the expansive local forests around Chiang Mai and see-ing many edible species in the markets, I knew there must be mushrooms out there somewhere! On a tip from a fellow traveler, I hired a taxi to take me up a nearby mountain called Doi Suthep. There is a beautiful Buddhist temple there, and I praised the mushroom spirits as I passed. This must have been the right thing to do because the woods behind the temple were loaded with mushrooms.

Unlike Southern Thailand, this area around Chiang Mai is more temperate in climate and less tropical in appearance—similar to our southern Appalachians. Ac-cordingly, I found different species of *Amanitas*, *Russulas*, *Lactarius*, *Mycenas*, and many others. Probably the most beautiful of my finds in this area was what looked like an *Amanita hemibapha*. At the right time in the eastern U.S. there is a similar one, *Amanita jacksonii*.

In the evenings, I networked with other travelers as well as local Thais. One of the people I met was a grade-school teacher named Parichad who taught English near Chiang Mai. We struck up a deal that if she showed me some remote places to hunt, I would talk (slowly in English) for some of her classes. We went to Thailand's highest mountain, Doi Inthanon, and I kept my agreement and talked to her students.

Temple on Doi Suthep, Chiang Mai

Foray with Thai teachers

Our deal went well and Parichad ar-ranged more exchanges with other teachers in schools north of Chiang Mai. With connec-tions set up for me, I traveled north to Chiang Dao and then northwest to a little hill town near the Burmese border. It was there that I found a stunning species of a forked fungus, (possibly *Cordyceps*) heavily laden with green spores (right). At the time of this writing, it is still unidentified.

Unidentified (TKF)

A Mycological Temple in Thailand

Over the years, I have had the honor of visiting the Thaitatgoon family who owns the Arunyik Mushroom Center outside of Bangkok. They have been and will continue to be a center of mycological influence and support in Thailand through their research, mushroom production, and community education.

Boonchock Thaitatgoon

Grampa Thaitatgoon

A young mycologist

Edible mushrooms grown in a vegetable garden

Close Call
Jinghong, China
July 1998

Close Encounters postcard

As I was exploring the hills around Chiang Mai, a fellow traveler suggested I go to China because it was so close. I went down to the local Chinese embassy to take my chances on getting a visa (it wasn't so easy then). Just in case it might help, I brought along some of my mushroom postcards. Good thing, as the lady there loved mushrooms.

Within a couple of days, I was on an airplane to Kunming without a map, guidebook, or phrase book. Sitting separately but near me on the plane were two younger western travelers. He was in Chinese studies at Yale, and she was taking a vacation from her work as an English translator in Taiwan. They found my situation amusing, and we all agreed to get a dorm-style room together in one of the nicer hotels.

The next day they helped me find a small dictionary, and though I could only use a few of its 3,000 translated words, it would soon help me in my mushroom quest. After checking the local weather, I was on another plane to the southern Hunan province town of Jinghong.

As I was wandering around Jinghong looking for lodging, I heard a voice from behind me say, "Can I help you?" As any experienced traveler knows, this could mean either real help or real trouble. However, the voice had a nice face, and my gut feeling was that this could be good. He introduced himself as Jon Tzu and said he worked across the street as a tour guide.

After talking awhile, I realized that while he was competent at English grammar, his spoken English was in need of some help. Fortunately he knew it too, and we made a deal. He would guide me to various places around the area to hunt mushrooms, and I would coach him in English pronunciation. First, he helped me find a hotel. It was one reflecting a bygone era of Communist bureaucrats and others of the elite who could afford it. My room was spacious, reasonably clean, and it had a television!

Over the next few days, we went on a few forays around the area and came up with several good finds. Some of

Cookeina tricholoma

Podoscypha petaloides

Callistosporium sp.

those were: a green "parrot mushroom" (pg. 50) Jon found on one of our hunts in an elephant preserve; a hairy cup fungus (*Cookeina tricholoma*); a paper thin bamboo mushroom I later identified as *Podoscypha petaloides*; and a group of bright yellow mushrooms, also in the bamboo, recently identified as a species of *Callistosporium*.

One day Jon and I took a long and bumpy bus ride up to a hill-tribe village. We then climbed up to a beautiful waterfall that looked like a scene from Shangri-La. As we walked up the trail I saw some yellow and wavy little sheets of spore-bearing surface. They were on a low bank near us and under the brush. I crawled into the bush on my hands and knees to get photo access to them. As I was preoccupied with maneuvering closer and into the right position, Jon started screaming in Chinese at the top of his lungs. I froze, and for good reason, as my head was about ten inches away from a deadly green tree snake. I slowly pulled my head back, retraced my approach, and maneuvered to get a shot of the mushrooms, *and* the snake. Jon appeared to be more shaken than I was (ignorance is bliss, I guess). I went on to have a good shoot there, and afterward we returned through several rice paddies followed by bumpy bus rides back to Jinghong.

After a few more days of mushroom hunting, I was ready to leave, but I felt that I owed Jon more than what he had gotten out of our deal. The morning of the day I left, I pulled my cassette recorder out of my pack and dictated all 3,000 words from my little dictionary (that's about one per second on a one-hour tape). As we said our farewells, I gave the tape and dictionary to him as a thank you for his help.

Dreamy waterfall

The snake that almost bit me

With Jon Tzu

Tarzan the Ape
Thailand
1998

Amanita rubrovolvata

I returned to Chiang Mai and was hunting again on Doi Suthep. After photographing a spectacular little *Amanita*, I took a path back through the forest. Over the path was a long, two-inch thick vine, hanging from the trees above. The vine had been cut so the bottom end was about three feet off of the ground.

After passing it at first and then thinking of the possibility of a missed opportunity, I went back to inspect it. It looked movie-set perfect. Though I hadn't seen anyone in the forest all day, I turned around to make sure no one was watching. I put down my gear and gave the vine a hefty tug to see if it could hold my weight. It was a little springy, but it passed the test, so I walked it back about fifteen feet, reached high, lifted myself up, and away I went.

I hadn't gone much further than where I found it when, with snaps and much clatter from above, I went down to the ground with forty feet of vine and branches falling all around and on top of me. Getting up with a few scrapes, I walked away thinking I should stick to my photography career.

Craterellus aureus, Thailand

Unidentified, China

Hygrocybe psittacina, China

Dictyophora multicolor, Thailand

Chasing the Rain

Marasmius sp., Malaysia

Dictyophora indusiata, Thailand

Cookeina sulcipes, Malaysia

Vanromburghia silvestris, Thailand

Indonesia

Sumatra, Log Notes
December 1998

Yesterday, I took a boat from Penang, Malaysia, to Medan, Indonesia, and after the customary hounding by money changers and taxi drivers, I headed straight for the little town of Berestaggi up in the mists of a volcano. Last night, as I got off the bus, I was met by a single guesthouse hawker (there are usually hordes). After I inquired about the rates, he took me up the hill to a converted Dutch-colonial house. A large room with a view of the Sibayak volcano ended up costing me 7,000 rupiahs! That translated to one U.S. dollar.

Today, as it looked green and mushroomy everywhere, I went up on the volcano. It was steamy with sulphur green and yellow caves in the hillside. On the way up, I found a few mushrooms, the prettiest of which was probably a witch's cap (*Hygrocybe conica*). It was a nice start to what I hope will be a fruitful adventure through this country.

Hygrocybe sp., Sumatra

Rice paddies, Bali

Chasing the Rain

The Titanic

The Titanic, the name a friend of mine calls my stomach of steel, is still afloat. In parts of Sumatra, you sit down to a plate of rice and a selection of small dishes that are all cold, spicy to very spicy, and mostly unidentifiable.

The ability to sit down and pick anything to eat around here makes one feel very fortunate. Not that I don't get pulled under occasionally. Yesterday I chose a dish that looked like green beans, but after dumping it all on top of my rice and braising the inside of my mouth, my Javanese bus mate explained "those are pure chilies."

It is certainly poetic injustice that the one thing the Titanic can't handle is a ride on the water. Tonight I take that boat from Sumatra to Java. I'm taking my Dramamine now.

Get down, Get Fungi! Bali, Log Notes December 1998

Well used wooden boats

Lake Maninjau, Sumatra

Traditional Minangkabau house design

Today I went to a temple area called Mungwi, known more as a local tourist trap with monkeys as the bait. I'm not too fond of looking like a tourist, so I went around to the back behind the temple where there were a lot of big old trees and mushrooms scattered around.

The challenge in hunting around monkeys is that they are mischievous, persistent, and can be very aggressive if they really want something you have (or just think you have). Although there were hundreds around the temple, they appeared to be fairly well behaved. I relaxed a bit and went on hunting mushrooms. As I scanned the forest floor, I found what looked like black trumpets. They were much like the ones back home, although these were greenish-yellow when young and matured to a smaller size than ours. In groups (photo, right), they were beautiful.

So, I lay on the ground, and I was enjoying taking photos of these "green trumpets." I noticed that while I was distracted by the mushrooms, I had been quietly surrounded by twenty to thirty monkeys. This might have been a completely harmless intrusion, but with monkeys, you just don't know! I slowly turned my head and looked around to try and assess their intentions. They seemed to be looking at my camera case.

I was determined not to have my film taken or my gear fingered and dropped from the trees. So, to get the advantage of surprise, I made a pre-emptive move. I sprang up and all the monkeys jumped back about ten feet. I laughed at their reaction, and I think they did too. Whether they knew it or not, that was my one and only move, so it was time for me to go!

Craterellus verrucosus

Monkey see, monkey take!

Boedijnopeziza insititia

Clavulinopsis sp.

Cordyceps sp.

Cyptotrama asprata

Chasing the Rain

Pleurotus djamor

Pluteus sp.

Microporus sp.

Borneo

Onward to Borneo
February 1999

Into the jungle

Few islands in the world possess the cachet of mystery and the exotic as Borneo. With that kind of reputation, I imagined they must have great mushrooms. I had to see for myself.

I flew in a small airplane from Semarang on the island of Java to Pangkalambun on Borneo, and then took a three-wheeled rickshaw to the little town of Kumai. An outpost for the mining and logging operations of the deep interior, Kumai also serves travelers headed for the Camp Leakey Orangutan Preserve. In a small office there, I obtained a permit to visit the preserve and met two couples who were doing the same.

We hit it off well and directly hired a klotok (a water taxi fit for Humphrey Bogart) for the next three days. With a classic putt-putt engine and slow, dreamy pace, we crossed the Kumai River the next morning and had a beautiful ride up the backwaters to the preserve. It was the best ten dollars I'd spent on transportation in a long time. That evening, the klotok dropped us off at the first camp, Tanjun Harapan, where rooms awaited us.

Klotok water taxi

On the boat trip to the camp we met Dr. Gede, a young volunteer veterinarian from Bali, who had come to treat the injured and orphaned orangutans. I was fascinated by his work, and he showed an interest in mine as well. With assistance from another preserve volunteer, he helped me find mushrooms to photograph. At one point, he asked if I would contribute something towards the orangutan's food and medical supplies. I said I would, and I offered to accompany him the next day to buy the supplies.

In the morning after waiting for the rain to stop, Gede and I set off by boat to Kumai and then to Pangkalambun. Before we left, I had told him that my contribution was predicated on cashing a traveler's check or using my last $100 bill. Considering the possibility of getting drenched from rain or waves on the way, I took the bill and left the traveler's checks and my passport at camp. I thought on Borneo, like everywhere else, my $100 bill would fetch a better rate than the check.

We went to the only bank in Pangkalambun where Gede did his best to translate the feeble explanation by the bank officer. When we left, explanation or not, I had lost 25% to the exchange rate! We went shopping anyway and got baby bottles, medicine, dish soap, wash pans, and food.

It was getting on towards evening, so we flagged down a speedboat already loaded with some miners who were headed back up the river to the their camps. With four of us crowded together on the rear bench, my lofty knees became too enticing for a tired young miner who laid his arms and head down on them and fell asleep. I was honored that he treated me as he would his friends.

Don't do the dishes until the orangutans are fed
Camp Leakey, Kalimantan
February 1999

Seeing the orangutans is an incredible experience. They are intelligent, clever, and strong, with arms like nimble lassoes. Keeping them out of mischief or from damaging the preserve's buildings, wires, and clotheslines is a vigilant, full-time job.

They are continually thinking of new ways to get at the stash of bananas hidden from them and for them. While I was there, one climbed onto the roof of the banana storehouse, tore a bunch of shingles off to make a gaping hole, and then poured a bucket of water inside as the not-so-amused ranger watched. We visitors got to laugh.

Although the orangutans frequently approach visitors to hold hands, cuddle, or climb onto, the staff advises against making any advances towards them. A threatened orangutan can launch into a scary display, or worse. It is also advised not to bring or show any signs of carrying food. If you have some, or they think you have some, they will grab whatever you have to get it. An average orangutan is strong enough to lift a backpack, and the person strapped to it, off the ground.

One afternoon, it was my turn to do the dishes. So, I headed down the long, plank walkway to the river with a pot full of dirty ones. Two rangers had joined me, and I soon realized that it wasn't just to keep me company. One of the mothers with her own infant and an adopted juvenile came through the bushes and up onto the walkway ahead of us. It was at that point I realized I was carrying the same pot the orangutans had stolen the day before. "Oh boy," I thought, "here comes trouble!"

The mother sneaked around the ranger in front of me and reached out to grab the pot, grabbing my arm instead as I pulled away. If she had gotten the pot, all the interested orangs would have inspected, licked, and played with everything in it, and there would probably have been broken plates and silverware all over the place.

The rangers shooed her away, and I came away with a scratch on my arm that bled a bright fluorescent red. The rangers and I contemplated whether it was the jungle juice (mosquito repellent) on my arms that made it that way, or whether I was really an alien from outer space. We continued down to the river and, alien or not, I did the dishes.

The Mozzies were Biting like Piranhas
Kalimantan
February 1999

Borneo has some of the most relentless mosquitoes I have ever encountered. With every inch of skin covered with jungle juice except the eyelids and nostrils, they attacked the eyelids and nostrils. It is usually hot and steamy there, so I wore a headband to help keep the sweat and repellent out of my eyes. If I stopped anywhere, it took only five seconds until there were a swarm of a hundred around me, and another five seconds brought hundreds more. For any serious photography under those conditions, timing was critical.

To simply look at something through the camera, fog had to be wiped off of the camera eyepiece and my glasses. To photograph something, I would do all of that again plus remove specks of dirt or insects off of the subject. Then I would take a mosquito break to lead them down the trail, hurry back, and do all the defogging again in hope of getting another shot. About the time when I started to feel artistic, the mosquitoes attacked again. The headband helped, but the mosquitoes bit through it and all my clothes as well.

My camp mates seemed bewildered by my sacrifice. I explained that the photos will last far longer than the bites, provided I got the film home and didn't bring malaria with it. At that point, home was about three weeks and 10,000 miles away.

Back to Borneo
February 2004

In 1999, I had visited the Indonesian part of Borneo, Kalimantan, after traveling through Sumatra, Java, and Bali. The northern states, Sarawak and Sabah, are part of Malaysia and were high on my travel wish list for years. In 2004, I got my chance to go there and look for mushrooms. I was well rewarded.

Once I got to Kuching in Sarawak, I traveled on a series of boats and small planes to the Kelabit plateau. It was cooler and more remote than the lowlands. After arriving, I hired a young guide named Golbart Pitan to help me with my search. Some guides understand quickly what I'm doing and what they can do to help me. Golbart *got it*, and as we went into the forest, he would find mushrooms ahead of me as I photographed the previous find.

One of the most beautiful mushrooms from Sarawak was an *Amanita hemibapha* var. *similis* (right, also on pg. 61).

Amanita hemibapha var. *similis*, Sarawak

Lentinus sp., The white ring on the cap could be *Hypomyces*

Another *Lentinus*, *L. similis* which was very stiff, like plastic

Unidentified, Sectioned

With Golbart's grandfather Pu'un Ulun

Cantharellus sp. My guide said they don't eat it

Durianiella
February 2004

My Kelabit guide Golbart and I were coming back from our mushroom hunting outing, and on the trail there was an odd thing that looked like a little durian. Now, if you don't know durian, it's very large, spiny, and odorous fruit that grows high up in its tree. When a durian ripens and falls, you don't want to be under it! I picked up the odd little earthball and then cut it open to see what was inside. The interior looked somewhat like a truffle but after a few minutes, the cut surface turned to a beautiful cobalt blue.

Since I had never seen anything like it before, I gave it an unofficial title of *Gautieria durianopsis*, in other words, looking like durian. I used the photo for years in my slide presentation "Fantastic Fungi of the World," without having a proper name for it. At one of my shows, mycologist Dr. Dennis Desjardin announced that it represented a new genus and species of fungi soon to be published with the official name *Durianiella rambutanispora*. Great minds think of durian!

Durian

Durianiella rambutanispora nom. prov.

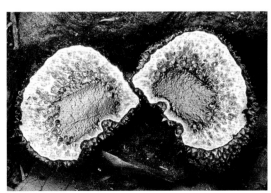

Staining blue after sectioning

Cantharellus sp., Sarawak

Chasing the Rain

Leptonia purpurea, Kalimantan

Amanita hemibapha var. *similis*, Sarawak

Calostoma insigne, Sabah

Unidentified, Sarawak

South Africa
& Zimbabwe

South Africa
January 2000

B y the beginning of 2000, I was convinced it was time to publish my first book, but I wanted to have more countries represented in it. I decided I would take the year to travel, and put the book together after that. Though I had never been to Africa, I had contacts in South Africa and Zimbabwe, so that's where I started.

After thirty hours of flying, sitting, and eating while strapped into my seat, I set my feet on African soil for the first time. I was just getting some money changed and ready to catch the bus to Pretoria when someone walked up to me and said, "Taylor?" In my jet lag haze I was surprised, mostly because the accent was not from a local South African but from an American. It was Dr. Robert Sinclair, in South Africa to study mycorrhizal fungi of the dune forests, who had graciously taken the time to pick me up unannounced.

On the road to Pretoria, he briefed me on the state of the country, the weather, and mushrooms. In a short while, I had a room in a home away from home with some friends of his. Soon after that I was making up for many hours of lost sleep.

The Drakensberg escarpment, South Africa

The next day, I was taken to lunch by two venerables of South African mycology, Professor Eicker of the University of Pretoria and retired Dr. Van der Westhuizen. We talked about several places to hunt mushrooms in Zimbabwe as well as South Africa. I was deeply honored by their graciousness and appreciation for my work and purpose. By the next morning I had a rental car and was headed toward northeastern South Africa and the Indian Ocean.

It was unseasonably dry there, but I did find a rare and spectacular stinkhorn called *Kalchbrennera corallocephala* (pg. 65). It cost me though, as I was stung by a wasp on the forehead and spent the good part of two days wondering if I would ever be able to open my eyelids again. After recovering from that little mishap, I drove through the Blyde River Canyon and then headed north to the South African border with Zimbabwe.

Stung in the forehead

Zimbabwe
January 2000

At the time I wanted to go to Zimbabwe, its government had not paid their fuel bill, and supplies were cut off at the pipeline through Mozambique. This meant that in order to get into Zimbabwe and return to South Africa, I had to find some gasoline containers and fuel to put in them. As I was the last to know about the fuel shortage, this was no easy task. After a few hours of driving around the towns near the border, I found three ten-liter plastic containers that (I hoped) wouldn't dissolve holding petrol. After more driving around, I found fuel and crossed into Zimbabwe with thirty liters of gas in the hatchback. Fortunately, it was raining and thereby safer for this liquid bomb sitting four feet behind me.

Felix

After a few stops on the way, I headed up into the Eastern Highlands around the town of Mutare. As Professor Eicker had advised me, this area was green and wet with lots of mushrooms to photograph. As I traveled I made a point of asking locals about traditional practices with mushrooms, and I recorded their stories on tape.

Rhizopogon sp.

One memorable foray was with a young Shona man named Felix. We found some *Amanitas* and an intriguing pink Bolete (pg. 64). On another walk, we found what looked like a common yellow *Rhizopogon*. Felix explained that when he was young and tending his father's cattle, he would find them, break them open, and eat the inside for a little nourishment and moisture. However, he was very nervous about touching the capped mushrooms. Apparently, that practice came with admonishing taboos.

Felix peels *Rhizopogon*

As I headed back toward South Africa, I used the gasoline I had been carrying. As I went, I left the containers by the side of the road for anyone to take. When I got back to Pretoria, I did a slide show for an astute audience at the University. They asked questions about my travels, hunts, finds, and future plans. Before the show, I had taken two rolls of slide film to a lab for processing. They contained photos of various mushrooms from my travels around South Africa including the wild-looking *Kalchbrennera corallocephala* stinkhorn I had found earlier. As a thank you for their help with my travel plans, I donated some slides of my finds and gave them a *Kalchbrennera* stinkhorn egg I had preserved for their herbarium.

Unidentified, South Africa

Hohenbuehelia aff. *mastrucata* sp., South Africa

Stropharia sp., Zimbabwe

Boletus sp., Zimbabwe

Mycena sp., Zimbabwe

Chasing the Rain

Kalchbrennera corallocephala, South Africa

Leucoagaricus sp., South Africa

Phlogiotis sp., South Africa

Mycena sp., Zimbabwe

Nigeria

Searching for the African Queen
May 2000

I had just returned from Zimbabwe and South Africa when I got a phone call from a young Nigerian mycologist named Omon Isikhuemhen. He had heard of me through Rytas Vilgalys, the mycologist I had met in Tasmania.

Omon had been working in Japan in DNA research, and

Isikhuemhen, Neda-san, Lockwood

he wanted to arrange an international foray to Nigeria to document species found there. He said that his boss in Japan, Hitoshi Neda, agreed to go. For me, an invitation to foray in Nigeria couldn't be passed up. We agreed to meet in Zurich and fly together to Lagos, Nigeria.

So, it was Omon, Hitoshi Neda and me. Using the Japanese honorative (*-san*) we soon became Omo-san, Neda-san, and Taylo-san. We were aided in our hunts by various scouts, most of whom were students from the University of Benin or locals from the villages. As we hunted, we found many recognizable and unrecognizable species. Names for mushrooms came up in various native languages as well as in Latin and English.

One of the highlights of the foray was searching for a mushroom that Omon said he used to see as a young child. With pink cap, gills, and stem, it would certainly be a candidate for my upcoming book *Treasures from the Kingdom of Fungi*. As the days passed, we traveled to the Akure zone, Edo north and through various villages and habitats. Everywhere we went there was something new and interesting to look at, talk about, and photograph, but no pink mushroom.

Termite mound

Then, after traveling to an area where we found spongy *Hydnums* wrapped around liana vines and *Leucocoprinus* caps speckled with red droplets, a call came through the forest, "Must see! Must see!" After winding my way closer, I knelt down as if to pay homage to the royal beauty we carefully photographed, collected, and called the "African Queen"—Omon's pink mushroom.

Lepista sp. (TKF)

Leucocoprinus birnbaumii (TKF)

Near the end of our stay, we went to Omon's village. It had been seven years since his last visit, and he had become an icon of local lore. There was no need to announce his return. Within a half hour of our arrival, there were a hundred people around his family home. The spontaneous celebration precipitated rounds of palm wine, toasts to Omon by the elders, and around the periphery, lots of talk about which mushrooms were edible and which were not. Songs and dancing by the women honored our visit to the village and Omon's return home.

Akpaja discussing edible and medicinal mushrooms

A good time was had by all

Some of the mushrooms we were looking for were any species of the *Termitomyces* genus (*T. microcarpus*, left, *T. clypeatus*, center). Termites cultivate the mycelium for food in underground "gardens," and when they abandon the nest, the mushrooms fruit. The photo on the left shows a mushroom and the mycelial garden. An abandoned garden (right) shows the remnants of mushroom stems (stipes) from previous fruitings. More termite mound fungi on page 27.

Mycena sp.

Unidentified

Lepiota sp.

Marasmius sp.

Unidentified

Geastrum saccatum

Anthracophyllum nigritum

Unidentified

Scytinopogon sp.

Amanita sp.

Cookeina sulcipes

Favolaschia sp.

Oudemansiella canarii

Marasmius sp.

All Nigeria

Lentaria sp.

Stop-over Foray
Switzerland
June 2000

After leaving Omon and Nigeria, Neda-san and I took the plane to Zurich for our flight connections. He would fly east to Japan, and I west to California. He had a thirteen-hour stopover and mine would be eight hours. That was a long time to wait for a long flight.

So, I thought we might conjure up something to do. We went downstairs to the information booth and asked if there was any place we could hunt mushrooms. Without hesitation, the attendant suggested a nice walk by a river and told us which two trains to catch. It was too easy. Fifty feet out of the airport were trains, and in a few minutes we were rolling through picturesque farmland and patches of forest. We connected to the second train, and within an hour of leaving the airport, we were walking along a tree-lined river which divided a small Swiss village.

Though it was misty and green there, June was not the best time to hunt mushrooms. However, it was a good place to get some exercise between flights and a great chance for Neda-san and me to get to know each other. Our token find was a small clump of *Coprinus micaceus*, but it was ancillary to our talk about cultures, travel, and mushrooming in other parts of the world.

The high point of the day was an unexpected offer by Neda-san, "Taylor, if you would like to come to Japan, please let me know." Without any hesitation, I returned, "Neda-san, I would love to come to Japan."

Through my minimal knowledge of Japanese culture, I knew that a direct offer and a direct acceptance carried a lot of weight. What I didn't expect was that over the next two months Neda-san would plan a complete Japanese tour for me, with guides, forays, and opportunities to present my slide show.

Swan and village, Switzerland

Indian Summer
June 2000

I had just returned from Nigeria. As I was decompressing from the trip, I reviewed my plan to get to as many countries as I could in 2000. I had some great shots for the upcoming book, and the year was only half over. High on my list was India.

I called my friend Rytas Vilgalys at Duke University. After telling him stories about Nigeria and his former student Omon, I mentioned I was thinking of going to India around the middle of July. I asked if he knew of anyone with experience in hunting mushrooms there. He thought for a second and said, "Well, you know, a Swiss-French mycologist I work with named Jean-Marc Moncalvo is planning to go there about the same time you are. Give him a ring." I called, and yes, he was planning to go the same time I was. Bingo! Jean-Marc said that he could use some company, so we planned to meet in Delhi.

The monsoons have arrived

Delhi street scene

Mcleod Ganj
July 2000

The morning after I arrived in Delhi, I met Jean-Marc, and we decided to get on the road. This meant tuk-tuk (motorized rickshaw), bus, and train rides, all heading up toward the foothills of the Himalayas to a little town called Mcleod Ganj.

We were told that the train left at 8:30, 10:30, 10:45, or 11:00. No one seemed to be sure. To be safe we got to the station at 8:00 a.m. People were collecting around the train cars, and it looked like there might be a crunch once the doors opened. An older Indian man sensed our naiveté and showed us what to do. Before the doors opened, he pushed up a window at the end of a car, climbed in head first (he was probably sixty-five), and took our bags through the window to claim our spot. After the conductor officially opened the doors, we took our seats and had a slow but beautiful ride from Puthankot to Kangra. Then, a few more bus rides took us to Mcleod Ganj.

The town was once a hill station where English military personnel could come and cool off. The area around Mcleod Ganj and Darhamsala is also the in-exile home of the Dalai Lama and many other Tibetan refugees. This makes for a great cultural mix of Indians, Tibetans, and foreign travelers. To celebrate our arrival, we found a Tibetan restaurant, discussed Tibetan philosophy with a young Englishman, and watched a lunar eclipse in progress over the Himalayas.

The next morning, while I was getting my photo gear ready, Jean-Marc was trying to arrange a meeting with some Indian mycologists. The day before, he took the trouble to bus down to a local university, but he couldn't get a straight answer about when his contact would arrive. So, frustrated and disappointed, he came back to Mcleod Ganj. I saw him just as he got off the bus, and took him to a great hunting spot I had found a little earlier. As he had come for mushrooms and not for battles with bureaucracy, it was just what he needed.

The woods there were loaded with fungi. Our timing was perfect. In an hour, we had found about thirty or more species and several specimens good enough for my photographic aspirations. We kept going until it started getting dark, then we went back to town and celebrated our first foray. Early the next morning, I woke up to a small earthquake and never got back to sleep. With the multi-story buildings there, all on the slopes, it's not the best place to experience an earthquake.

After a couple of days Jean-Marc got a message that one of his contacts was coming up to Mcleod Ganj to see us. A nice and nicely dressed man named Ashok arrived the next day with the intent of doing a little hunting. After lunch, we all drove down the hill to a pine forest we had

Mcleod-Ganj

Jean-Marc with *Ganoderma lucidum*

seen earlier. As Ashok hung out by the side of the road, we looked for mushrooms and kept coming up with new ones. Occasionally, locals would walk by and show interest in what we were doing. One was a deaf-mute who kept waving her hands (or probably signing) and grunting in delight each time we brought a new mushroom up the hill.

Our energy must have been infectious because Ashok eventually started climbing the hills and finding mushrooms with us. By the end of the day, he agreed to come back up a few days later. Then word must have spread. A student that Jean-Marc had been trying to reach called the next day and said that he was coming too. He took the day-and-a-half trip to meet us, and soon we were all out in the woods finding and identifying fungi. Score one for the infectious spores of enthusiasm!

Jean-Marc collects as a local watches

A young Tibetan refugee and poet, Pelshang, explains traditional uses of *Ganoderma lucidum* (in his hand and above)

Back to Delhi
Log Notes
July 2000

I am back in Delhi and on my way to Bangkok tonight after having a great time with Jean-Marc. This trip has been really good partly due to his scientific knowledge and willingness to share it.

I spent thirteen hours on the bus coming down from the mountains. The trip was punctuated by various breakdowns and other mishaps. The number of cars and trucks driving in the night without rear lights is unusually high here. As I was imagining some sort of accident, a truck-trailer rig (with no lights, of course) pulled in front of us at about 20 m.p.h. To avoid hitting the truck our driver careened the bus onto a raised divider. He struggled to keep the bus barely upright as the women inside screamed. You can bet that woke everyone else up. Then the only way the driver could get the bus off the divider was to head into the fast lane of the opposing traffic. It was a few hairy minutes of driving the wrong way until he found a break in the divider and crossed over to the correct direction of traffic. Just another day on the road.

Amanita angustilamellata

Lepiota sp.

Gomphus sp.

Auriscalpium vulgare

Japan

While I was in India, Neda-san had been planning my Japanese mushroom tour, unbeknownst to me. A few weeks after I returned home, he emailed to say that my trip to Japan was all set up. He works in one of many connected forestry research centers, and he used his connections to arrange my tour. As I was used to hard traveling, I became a little spoiled having everything set up for me. Honor has a special meaning in Japan, and I was *honored*.

Welcome to Hokkaido
Sapporo
September 2000

Pholiota sp.

Oudemansiella mucida

Amanita sp.

Ten thousand mushrooms! The first day!
My first morning in Japan, I awoke in the forestry center guesthouse to a six-course breakfast prepared by the resident cook. After all the appropriate *oishii des* (it's delicious) and *arigato gozaimas* (thank you), I walked up the hill to find the spruce forest floor glowing with mushrooms. Actually there were probably more than ten thousand, but who's counting?

After a couple of days in Sapporo my host Takehiro Yamaguchi and I took a trip around southern Hokkaido. This included a club foray in O-numa, two nights stop-over in Muroran, a foray there and my slide show in both places. In Muroran, I was hosted by a kind and lively man, Yoichi Nishihara. He had a jolly friend who kept telling me, through his chuckles, that he used to be a kamikaze pilot in WWII! It took me years to get it.

The event in O-numa was very upscale with a foray, a great dinner, my slideshow after-wards, and another foray the next day. We found a large number of species, and my best find was a *Tricholoma bakamatsutake*. After lunch, I traveled to Muroran in a bus full of beer drinking, singing, Japanese mushroom hunters.

After that, I returned to the guesthouse in Sapporo and had dinner with Izawa Masa (Japan's eminent fungi photographer) as the rain made mushroom music on the roof.

Fumiko Sawada

Boletus violaceofuscus
by Fumiko Sawada

With Yoshiyuki Suga and Eizan Konno

With Izawa Masa

Tricholoma bakamatsutake

The Cuckoo
Chiba

After a foray in Chiba, I presented another slide show, which was received even better than the previous ones. At a party afterwards, I shared many toasts with one of Japan's eminent mycologists, Dr. Hongo. At another party, I played (on a battery-powered electric violin) one of my old showstoppers, "the Cuckoo," to all the clapping and cheering I might have expected back in my rock-and-roll days.

2000年度観察会報告-p3
テイラーさんのバイオ
懇親会会場では、近田さ
ンでアイリッシュ民謡
Treasures fro
テイラーさんのサ
http://www.fun
Chiba Mushroom Club newsletter

Akihiro Sawada, Toshimitsu Fukiharu, Ryoko Onuma, Dr. Hongo, Taylor, Hiroko Fukiharu, Morishige Shimabukuro, Etsuzo Sano

Amanita aff. *longistriata*

Chasing the Rain

One of my hosts, Tsutomu Hattori, took me to a park where we found a couple of mushrooms I'd not seen before. Above: *Lyophyllum fumosum* and left: *Omphalotus guepiniformis*. The latter is bioluminescent, but we found it just before the last train left so we couldn't wait for dark to see it glow.

Sleeping in the Volcano
Kumamoto

The first couple of days in Kumamoto were sunny and beautiful, but there were no mushrooms. I hunted around the forestry research center, and although I found a few saprophytes on the local logs, it was still too warm for much else.

That evening, I presented a slide show for the Kumamoto Mushroom Club. I was surprised and touched by the large number of club members there. Over the previous two years, I had sent them several mushroom postcards, and they responded with their presence. The show went over very well, and I was happy it was a hit.

The next day, Neda-san and I headed toward the Kirishima National Park and mountains. Although it was dry there, we found enough mushrooms to call the afternoon a success. Afterwards, we headed for the hotel, dinner, and the baths. These were all situated in an old volcanic caldera which was still active with newer volcanoes all around, steam vents, and plenty of hot water for the bathers.

The bath thing was a little bit touchy as many Japanese are not accustomed to having foreigners in their special place. Neda-san assured me that it would be okay, and it was. Doing the baths solidifies friendship and I was honored to be invited.

We went off in the morning to do some more hunting. We had been out a couple of hours when I found an odd, greenish thing sticking out of the ground. Was this a mushroom, a tree stem, or the chewed-off stalk of wild asparagus? It was a mushroom, all right. Neda-san said that he had known about it, but after forty years of mushroom hunting he had never seen a *Pseudotulostoma japonicum* in the wild!

Pseudotulostoma japonicum (above and below)

Amanita virginioides

Chasing the Rain

Phlogiotis sp.

Stropharia aeruginosa

Unidentified

Boletellus emodensis

Burma

Kalaw
August 2002

Mt. Popa monastery

A t one point, the distance I could go between shaded rests was about fifty feet or one minute, whichever came first. "I will never do this again," I was grumbling to myself as I huffed and puffed slowly up the steps carved into the red clay. I was following a hill-tribe guide and an English-speaking Bamar guide named Mr. Win.

Our old friend and foe the Sun was nearly perpendicular, as it tried to cook the back of my neck preparing it for the mosquitoes to feast upon if I ever made it to shade again. I was ready to call it off as that elusive "top" looked increasingly like the oasis of the desert. I don't object to knocking myself out for mushrooms, mind you, but I was not ready to do so just to end up at some hill-tribe tourist trap.

So with each step, and thoughts about my first and maybe last heart attack up in the middle of nowhere, I was feeling a bad mood coming on. In my darkest hour the trail was starting to get a little easier, but there were fewer and fewer shade trees. All I could see were crops of corn, tea, and whatever else grew there to be hauled down to the market every five days.

Temples at Bagan

inally, as we rounded the top, my puffing slowed, and we could see rolling hilltops with a few houses, some more crops, and patches of forests and bamboo groves. I was starting to feel a little better.

Then I noticed some encouraging signs. There was no plastic refuse around the houses. The kids and adults came out, acknowledged us and waved back as I waved at them. Although they spoke a different language amongst themselves, a few adults responded positively when I gave them the ubiquitous Bamar hello, *mengalaba*. So at this point, even if I didn't find all the mushrooms that the hill-tribe guide had raved about, at least I wasn't dead!

We were finally on level ground. As we kept walking my spent legs had only to deal with our momentum, and not gravity, in the thinning air. As I started coming out of my funk, I said to myself, "This place is beautiful." It was indeed clean, remote, and gorgeous. I started to think that we just might find some mushrooms.

Mr. Win's first suggestion was to go to the Buddhist monastery. These areas are usually off limits to logging, firewood cutting, or anything else of that nature, but not mushroom hunting. I was starting to feel religious! So, we walked through the bamboo groves in the middle of the village and into an exceptionally clean and well-kept monastery yard. There we immediately enlisted a couple of eager young monks to go up into the pine forest with us to see what we could see. We found *Russulas*, *Amanitas*, *Gomphus*, and many others.

After a few photos to commemorate our early good fortune, we spread out and up toward more shaded areas. Then as the scope of our find became clear, I remembered my words "one to five hours" to my driver who was waiting down the hill where we started. We were already three hours into this and just getting into gear.

After an afternoon of great hunting and feeling guilty about leaving my driver to bake in his car, I decided to stop mushrooming for the day and head back down the hill. Smiles all around as I let them know how pleased I was, and gave the village guide a whopping 2,000 kyat ($2) thank you.

Our guides with a group of *Gomphus* sp.

Asking about local favorite edibles

Hunting on the way to work

Mushroom hunter with *Termitomyces* sp.

A very different looking *Agaricus, A. crocopeplus*

Roadside mushroom shrine

Lepiota sp.

Laccaria sp.

Amanita sp.

Boletus emodensis

Chasing the Rain

Strobilomyces sp.

Amanita hemibapha

Cantharellus sp.

Strobilomyces velutipes

Burma   85

Europe

Spain
October 2003

I arrived in Europe during one of the worst droughts in their history. Though it had been hot and dry all summer, I thought October would be a safe time to expect rain and mushrooms. Not necessarily so. It didn't rain before or anytime during my stay. But I found a lot more than I expected considering the circumstances.

Before I arrived, a Catalan e-mail friend Jordi Rodon, had suggested I head to the little town of Setcases in the mountains of northeastern Spain. They would be having their yearly *Festa del Bolet* the day after I arrived in Madrid. Though Europe was still hot and dry, Setcases, being higher in elevation, would be a great place to start.

When I arrived there it seemed like they had no connection to the drought. They had tables full of identified species and mushrooms for sale. There were mushrooms in the stores and mushrooms on all the menus. I had brought a dozen of my *Treasures* books and within an hour of my arrival all books were sold, save for one to travel with. Within two hours of my arrival, I was out hunting with a group from the festival. It was touching

Drought stricken corn fields, Spain

Setcases Mushroom Festival

Carcasonne, France

to see how quickly our shared interest made us friends.

As I was leaving, they suggested I head west towards *Pais Vasco* (Basque country) to an area called Irati. I had to ask for directions often, because I couldn't find it on any map. After I got there I understood why. The place was loaded with

Rut Mir with *Amanita caesaria*, Cataluña

mushrooms. There were a few pickers here and there, but not enough to keep me from finding lots of *Boletus edulis* and a few chanterelles as well as *Flammulina velutipes*, *Amanita phalloides*, *Oudemansiella mucida*, and many others.

After a few more days of back and forth over the Pyrenees between France and Spain, I stayed with some new friends that I met at the Setcases Festa. The next day two of them, Guillem and Rut, took me up into the cork trees to look for a favorite *Amanita* of theirs. In America we have a similar variety named *Amanita jacksonii*. There is a another similar one in Asia named *Amanita hemibapha*. But the one we were looking for and found was the European original, *Amanita caesaria*.

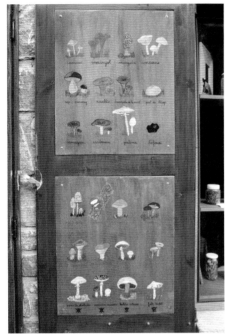

Window shutter in Setcases, Spain

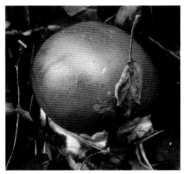

Amanita caesaria, Cataluña, Spain

Mushroom postcards help break down language barriers, Italy

Fresh mushrooms dispayed in a French pharmacy

What drought? Italy

Local mushroom fair display, France

Jewelry display in France

After several days in the Pyrenees, I awoke in the hills of Cataluña and thought about getting over to Italy. If all worked out, the next day I would make a surprise visit to a group of American and Italian friends who were on a mushroom foray in Asti, in northern Italy. Back in America a couple of weeks before I had scribbled down the name of the restaurant where they were supposed to be. I had mused that, if and when I got there, I'd just ask someone where it was. Sounds easy, right? *No Signore!*

As I was cashing some traveler's checks in France, I realized I had lost a day somewhere. The dinner was that night, not the next night! Oh well. If I made it, fine. If I didn't, fine. But I was determined to give it a shot. I got into Italy and sped through a zillion tunnels. Though it would take a lot longer than it looked on the map, I hoped that I could get to Asti on time. Sure enough, somewhere around seven o'clock (dinner was at eight) I pulled into Asti. I knew immediately I was going to have problems, as this was no quaint little Italian town. However, I had gotten there, and I was going for it.

First, I asked a taxi driver for directions in the chopped up Italian/Spanish/English mix I blurted out. My scribbled writing certainly didn't help at all, as I deciphered it to mean "Ristorante Romero." The taxi driver tried to help but could only reply, "What part of the city?" "Oh boy," I thought, "I'm in trouble again." I got back in my car and started driving around looking for restaurant signs, as if there was ever a chance of finding it that way. After a few loops through mazes of tiny one-way streets, I stopped to catch my wits and talk to a couple that had an old and inviting bookstore. They too were very helpful, looking in the phone book, the tourist guide, calling someone to ask, but *no ristorante, no cigarillo.* I decided to give this up and head back to the main road, so I could get up into the hills for mushroom hunting tomorrow.

On the way out of town, I happened to drive by an Internet cafe. Quickly pulling over and parking on the sidewalk ("When in Rome . . ."), I walked through the restaurant to a room filled with huge overstuffed couches and one old computer in the corner. Wasting no time, I did searches for Albert Casciero, the leader of the foray, and Ristorante Romero or any schedule that might have been posted. I found schedules for forays in 2001 and 2002 but none for 2003. Almost ready to give up on all this for the second time, I was thinking the group must be having their second glass of wine. I decided as a last try to search for "ristorante, Asti." In one of the three hits that came up was "Ristorante Rovero" (not *Romero*) in San Marzanotto. BINGO! I didn't know which way to go but at least I thought I had the right place! Quickly paying a hefty six Euros for twenty minutes there, I asked for and got directions to the district known as San Marzanotto.

In a few minutes, I was on the outskirts of town, but no lights, no ristorante, no nothing. Heading back quite disappointed, I came upon two younger Italian couples who were standing outside another restaurant, so I decided to try asking them. I made a U-turn in the road, which was just too small for my car. The car went up onto the curb very easily, but when it came down I heard a crunch. "Ouch," I said and got out to take a look at what might be left of the wheel cover. The wheel cover was fine, but what wasn't fine was my tire, which now was singing a light, steady, "sssssssssssss." The clock was ticking.

I went over to the other side of the street to ask the couples where I might find San Marzanotto. They were quite inebriated but ready to help. One woman weaved over to look at my tire "sssssssssss" as her mate drew a very respectable map (considering the condition he was in). The good news was that it was the same direction that the cyber café guy had indicated. But now I had another clue. I was supposed to look for Tortino.

Then I jumped into my car and with my tire going "sssss-wwwww-sssss" down the road, I headed back toward the edge of town and into the darkness. Going over the same bridge I had crossed before, I realized the signs that were supposed to be there, were not! "That's it! I've got to stop this and find a place to change my tire and get on down the road!" However, as I started to head out of town with my tire still singing "sss-www-sss-www-sss," I saw a little side road with a sign that said "Tortino." I still didn't know where San Marzanotto was, but my tire was not totally flat yet, so I gunned it down the road.

After about three miles I came to a little group of buildings with a small hotel. I ran out and up to the door. Lights on, but nobody home! I ran back to the car and went farther down the road "sssss-wwwww-sssss-wwww," and although I went beyond the five kilometers that should have gotten me there, I saw a sign that read, "San Montenegro." It didn't sound right, but it was all I had to go on at that point. So gun it I did up to a little town that was definitely shut down for the night. "This is ridiculous! I've got to find somewhere to change my tire and stop this nonsense." I turned around, headed back toward Asti, and just as I was passing the little hotel (with lights on and nobody home), I saw a small sign on a dark, dirt road which read "Rovero." "This has got to be the place!"

Up the road in the dark I went, certain that my tire must have been flat. But the smell of victory was in the air! In a couple of minutes, I came to a group of buildings that looked like a small winery. And there on the other side of the road was a clear sign of success, a tour bus! Now quite confident that I had found the spot, I parked my car next to the bus, forgot about the tire, and headed into the compound.

There were some Italian men standing outside the door. As I pointed inside I asked:
"Americanos?"
"Si."
"Albert Casciero?"
"Si."
"Excellente!!!!!"

Some of the men outside spoke English, so I explained that I knew the people inside, but they had no idea I was coming. They were game for some fun, so one went inside and explained that they had a little surprise for the dinner party. I followed and as I knew most of them, they were surprised!

They invited me to sit down for the remainder of the meal as I told them of the whole ordeal getting there. They told me that the Italian bus driver got lost trying to find the place, by daylight. Through the rest of the dinner I explained several times how my tire was losing air on the way, and that I would have to fix it after dinner. It must have seemed like I was exercising some poetic license in that regard until after all were fed and laughing our way to the parking lot, there was my tire, flat as a pancake.

I insisted that everyone should just get into the bus, and I would fix the tire myself. But Albert would not hear of it. So I drove, rim on rubber, a few yards to the pavement. Albert, Gerry Sheine, the bus driver, and I changed my tire by the light of camera flashes and flashlights with the whole rest of the dinner party merrily watching.

Now well fed and with four good tires, I said my thanks to my hosts who were headed to their hotel. I, thinking more about hunting mushrooms tomorrow than sleeping tonight, headed north and up into the Alps.

Fixing the flat tire by flashlight

Flammulina velutipes, Spain

Laccaria amethystina, Italy

Boletus edulis, France

Chasing the Rain

Oudemansiella mucida, Spain

Amanita phalloides, Spain

Unidentified, Switzerland

Stropharia aeruginosa, France

Tibet

Summer Grass, Winter Worm
July 2005

I was showing my work at the Fungus Federation's yearly fair in Santa Cruz, California, when a tall, young man named Todd Stagnaro came up and started chatting. He mentioned he was learning Mandarin Chinese as well as a couple of dialects of Tibetan. He also said that if I felt so inclined, he would be interested in a mushroom hunt with me in some remote parts of Tibet. Wow, I thought, what an opportunity! Within a few months I went from planning to plane tickets to packing, and we met in Xining, China, to embark on our journey.

Above and below: Jyekundo Horse Festival

We timed the trip so we could see the Jyekundo Horse Festival as well as the *Cordyceps* markets in some of the more remote villages. Todd had planned that we would travel south from Jyekundo to the sacred lake Yilhun Lhatso, Manigango, Derge, and return. There would be several possibilities to hunt for mushrooms on the way south and then later on the trip back.

Tibetan yaks

I was very interested in the culture and local industry that revolves around *Cordyceps sinensis*. Both Xining and Jyekundo had large outdoor markets with buyers, sellers, and onlookers. They were very attentive to the quality, size, and price of the highly sought after fungus-infected moth larvae (right and pg. 94).

On our return trip from Derge, we had hired a car and driver to take us back to Manigango and the nearby Lake Yilhun Lhatso. We had just come over a 16,000 ft. pass when we saw many groups of Tibetan Buddhists standing by the roadside in the rain. We found out that there was a High Lama coming our way. Many of these groups would slow us down and look into our car just to see if the Lama was with us. Two western travelers were not exactly what they expected, and one group got a big surprise. Todd, a practicing student of Buddhism and a very competent Tibetan-style throat singer, got out of the car, spoke a little Tibetan to them, and then belted out a prayer chant. They all exploded into smiles and laughter.

Cordyceps sinensis sidewalk market

Todd (far left) entertains Tibetans waiting in the rain for a High Lama

Todd Stagnaro examining a yet-to-be-identified *Boletus*

Tents at the Jyekundo Horse Festival

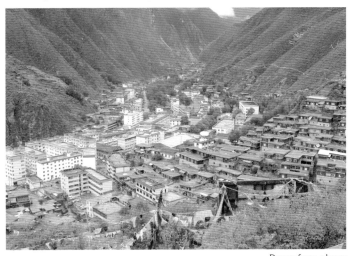

Derge from above

Cordyceps sinensis (above) is a fungus which infects the ghost moth in its larval stage. It is cited in ancient Tibetan literature and is one of the most revered elements of traditional Chinese medicine. Once it has been harvested and dried, it becomes an important commodity in Tibet (and gets its own billboard, above center). The Tibetan name is *yartsa gunbu,* translated into English as "summer grass, winter worm."

Above and below: *Sersha (Floccularia luteovirens)* is a favorite mushroom of Tibet.
A Tibetan saying goes: "Why eat yak when sersha is on the table?"

The smile says it all!

Dried *Ganoderma lucidum* in the market

Above and below: Sellers and buyers of *Sarcodon* sp. (Hawk's wing) in Derge

Derge, Tibet

Mushroom soup

Dried *Auricularia* sp.

Public toilet in Xining, China

Manigango
August 2005

Todd said that good karma was with us, and he was right. The only bus going to Manigango for the next week was parked outside our rooms, and was owned by a friend of the hotel manager. When the driver showed up, our packs went into the luggage compartment. We got in and headed to the bus station where everyone got out again. A tense hour or so passed as the booked passengers took their berths, and we waited to see if we were really "in" or "out." In the end, it was Todd, a Tibetan college girl, two young monks, and me in the back of the sleeper bus, five across, upper level.

By the time the bus got rolling, both aisles were filled with extra passengers

By some blessing of fate, I got a window berth, which gave me a little extra room. More importantly, being next to the window gave me some control over letting the cigarette smoke out and keeping the diesel smoke from coming in. However, the back of the bus is the worst for travel sickness, so I took a Dramamine without thinking about it. Speaking of motion, at one point in 400 kilometers of bumpy roads, the five of us levitated at least six inches, knocking my elbow into the upper window jamb. I was happy that at least I landed in the same berth.

After eighteen hours, three tire repairs, and other mysterious stops, we arrived in the dark at the little truck-stop town of Manigango. At the bus stop, an offer of accommodation in a dorm room behind the corner shop seemed a better option than hiking up the road in the dark and rain.

The place looked comfortable enough. Several beds lined the walls of a very woodsy room lit by a typical one-candlepower light bulb. There were old, striped, plastic tarps loosely nailed to the low ceiling, and a sliding wooden door and doorway that were not nearly high enough for either Todd or me. After a dinner of "pour the hot water over the noodles in plastic," we went to—what should have been—sleep.

Now next to this place was a huge, steel, three-sided billboard that (except for the steel frame) was completely in tatters with a large sheet of metal dangling and banging against the steel frame in the wind. Other than that, bed okay, comforter good, extra blanket nearby, lights out, and now what? Rats.

They used the plastic on the ceiling to get to different parts of the house, and their main highway was right over my head. At least there weren't holes in the plastic to pass droppings onto my face. After a couple of hours, the rats finished their running around, and I fell asleep, but not for long! Then, it was dogtime!

The goal was to bark as many times as possible as fast as possible until something louder took over. One o'clock, two o'clock, three o'clock, bark! I must have gotten some sleep though because, according to my watch, it was 4:30 a.m. when a woman and two or three men came chattering into the front room next to ours. That covered the dog for about fifteen minutes and then one of the men went out and started up the one-cylinder *Mao-plow** tractor, conveniently parked next to our only window.

**Mao-plow* is the name I use for an engine and accessory system from China that can become, among other things, a tractor, pick-up, or plow

After about fifteen minutes of the tractor noise, they all disappeared with the fading "putt-putt" of the engine. As that receded, the dog took over again. Just as I had gotten used to him, the rats returned overhead, searching for breakfast before the owners opened up the kitchen. Sometime after the sun came up, both Todd and I gave up any hope of sleeping.

Sleep and accommodation mishaps notwithstanding, it would turn out to be the start of the best day so far. We spent it at the beautiful and sacred Lake Yilhun Lhatso which had many mushrooms sprinkled around large, carved mani stones.

Remember to breathe!
Lake Yilhun Lhatso
August 2005

Photographing an *Amanita* at 14,000 ft.

At 14,000 feet, life flourishes here where most American mountains peak out. It is clean and quiet, the lake is green and cold, and there are mani stones all around the area. It is obvious why the Tibetans consider this a sacred lake. It is really beautiful here.

To add to the beauty, there were plenty of mushrooms. Hunting them meant a lot of energy output and oxygen input. As I was puffing from one mushroom to another, Todd pointed out that two-thirds of the Earth's breathable oxygen was below us. That meant you had to take three deep breaths where you were used to taking one. If I got down on the ground to look at or photograph a mushroom, I would have to think about my breathing before I tried to get up. "In, out, in, out, in, out. Okay, I think I'm ready now."

Mani stone by Lake Lhatso

Boletus sp.

Lepiota sp.

Sarcodon sp.

Chasing the Rain

Phlogiotis sp.

Panaeolus antillarium

Phaeocollybia sp.

Clitocybe sp.

North America

Bringing It All Back Home

I have been asked more than once, "What are your favorite mushroom hunting locations?" While that might seem like a simple question, the answer is not. Every location has rare and exotic mushrooms to someone else halfway around the world. While I love to bring my exotic mushroom photos back to America, I also love showing our exotic mushrooms to others when I travel. The bottom line is this: anywhere you live on earth, you could have beautiful examples of the fungal kingdom in your own backyard.

That being said, this chapter is devoted to *our* beautiful, exotic, and sometimes tasty mushrooms.

As for my favorite locations, those are the ones that I haven't been to yet. There, both at home and abroad, is where I will find new treasures.

Bringing film and stories home

Medea Minnich with *Cantharellus tubaeformis*, California

Craterellus cornucopioides
Massachusetts

A hat will do

Yanti Heath uses her parasol
North Carolina

Michigan woods

Climacodon septentrionale, Massachusetts

Chlorophyllum molybdites, Virginia

Todd Elliott photographing Austroboletus betula

Whatever it takes

Hen-of-the-Woods
September 2004

This trip was the first time I had ever flown anywhere just for a single species of mushroom. The honor and effort was for *Grifola frondosa*, also known as hen-of-the-woods or by its Japanese name, *maitake*. This coveted mycomedicinal is not found in the wild on the west coast, but that year it was abundant in the Midwest and Northeast. The timing was good, as I needed some new shots for my photo catalog.

My hunts were arranged by two friends and excellent scouts, Roy Reehil in upstate New York, and Elinoar Shavit in Massachusetts. We kept in almost daily contact so I could time my trip well, and when they said, "Now," I flew. They found choice specimens and then led me to them to archive and document their subtle grace. When I arrived in Massachusetts, I was treated to a simultaneous fruiting of hundreds of *Grifola frondosa*.

Grifola frondosa, (hen-of-the-woods), New York

Getting the shots

Medea with Sandy Sheine, Michigan

From somewhere in upstate New York

All: *Grifola frondosa*, Massachusetts (above and opposite)

Road sign in Oregon

"Mushrooms, you soon discover, are wild things in every way, beings pursuing their own agenda quite apart from ours. Which is why 'hunting,' rather than harvesting, is the mycophile's preferred term of art."

—Michael Pollan
from *The Omnivore's Dilemma*

Lorenzo Simi, California

Medea with Chanterelles, California

Boletus edulis, California

Cantharellus formosus, Washington

Craterellus cornucopioides, California

Chris Sterling slicing up *Boletus edulis* for drying, California

Paul Stamets blessing Dusty Yao's *Hericium*, Washington

Chasing the Rain

Peg Boulay with *Boletus edulis*, Oregon

Boletus edulis, California

Boletus aereus, California

Boletus edulis, California

North America   105

Morel Hunting in America

Morchella esculenta, Michigan

Nothing in the world of mushrooming in America causes more anticipation and excitement than one particular Ascomycete genus named *Morchella*. This is all for good reason as they are considered choice edibles, are fun to hunt, often very fruitful, and easy to identify.

It took me years before I found my first morels. There are several reasons for this: they didn't grow where I lived; I tried to find them without experienced help; and when I hunted for them, I was looking in the wrong places. These factors are all important to the social aspect of morel hunting culture. It makes one seek out others to learn from unless you are fortunate to have someone teach you as a child.

Because of these factors (and our general nature of wanting to hunt, gather, and eat) morel hunting, especially in the Midwest, has now become the foremost single social event of mushrooming in America. I have been fortunate to see its morel mania in full force for three seasons.

With Tom Nauman of Morel Mania

The Three Musketeers, *Morchella esculenta*, Illinois

Morchella semilibera, Illinois

After a two-hour hunt, hundreds of morels wait to be weighed at the Illinois State Morel Mushroom Hunting Championship in Henry, Illinois

Bringing home the goods, Michigan

Midwest divining rods

Morchella esculenta, Illinois

Morchella tulipifera, Kentucky

Morchella angusticeps, Michigan

Elinoar Shavit with *Morchella esculenta*, Illinois

Morchella esculenta, Illinois

Chasing the Rain

A six-pack of morels, Wisconsin

Morchella esculenta, Michigan

Champion hunter Roger Thurow, Michigan

E ven when conditions are not optimal, and you feel lucky if you find a few morels, a good hunter can come out with hundreds within a couple of hours. This level of expertise, by those who have it, is tested and rewarded at many Midwest morel-hunting contests.

There is a lot of folklore about morels' first appearance in the spring. Depending on whom you talk to, you might hear, "when the dandelions have lost half of their seeds," "when the laurel is in full bloom," or "when the oak leaves are as big as squirrels' ears." And, if the redbuds and lilacs are blooming, you better get your basket out today!

Time to hunt!

In the West though, from California to Alaska (pgs. 110-111), morels are far more prolific in the springtime after a forest fire. When conditions are right, they can be seen not in the hundreds, but in the millions. That still doesn't make them easy to find, and if you're like I was, you'll probably need someone to show you how.

The best part of morel hunting is that from parents and grandparents to children, you can share the anticipation and the hunt, and then the bounty simmering in the pan.

Get your basket out!

Morchella esculenta, Michigan

Morchella esculenta, Illinois

Morchella sp., Oregon

Morchella sp., Oregon

Morchella sp., Oregon

Morchella sp., Montana

Chasing the Rain

Fuzzy Foot morels, Montana

Fungal Boogieman Larry Evans, Montana

Morchella sp., Montana

Morchella sp., Montana

Lactarius indigo, Pennsylvania

Xerula furfuracea, Vermont

Unidentified, Quebec

Amanita muscaria var. formosa, Quebec

Chasing the Rain

Leccinum atrostipitatum, Quebec

Flammulina velutipes, Michigan

Cortinarius iodes, Pennsylvania

Lentinellus cochleatus, North Carolina

Chasing the Rain

Austroboletus betula, North Carolina

Strobilomyces floccopus, North Carolina

Pseudocolus fusiformis,
North Carolina

Pholiota squarrosa, North Carolina

Amanita muscaria, Oregon

Chasing the Rain

Gymnopilus spectabilis, Washington

Albatrellus ovinus, Oregon

Cortinarius violaceus, Washington

Psilocybe squarrosa, Oregon

Pluteus atromarginatus, California

Chasing the Rain

Armillaria mellea, California

Hygrocybe sp., California

Gomphus floccosus, California

Cortinarius vanduzerensis, California

North America   119

Polyporus tenuiculus, Puerto Rico

Dictyophora indusiata, Puerto Rico

Podoscypha petaloides, Puerto Rico

Chasing the Rain

Xylaria sp., Puerto Rico

Phillipsia domingensis, Puerto Rico

Unidentified, Puerto Rico

Lentinus sp., Puerto Rico

North America   121

Aseroe rubra, Hawaii

Chasing the Rain

On the Stinkhorn Trail
Hawaii
January 2007

It hadn't been since the *Grifola* shoot that I booked a flight for just one mushroom. For an upcoming project, I needed a good photo of *Aseroe rubra* and from all I could gather (if it rained) they would be out. Moreover, if I didn't find any there was a consolation prize, it was Hawaii!

So, Medea and I planned, booked the flights, and flew over there, even though I knew the odds were stacked against me. It was unusually dry. My contact, Dr. Don Hemmes from the University of Hawaii, couldn't be there to show me around. And, all I had to go on was some information I had scribbled down from a phone call to him. Once again, I had set up a mushroom hunt on a whiff and a prayer, and it wasn't looking too promising. However, as we slept the first night in Hawaii, it started raining the kind of rain that stinkhorns love.

In the morning, I did manage to contact one of Don's students, Russell Shioshita, who offered to show me some hunting spots. But after a day of much driving and searching, we came up with no *Aseroe rubra*.

The next day I found a different stinkhorn, *Dictyophora cinnabarina*, through another tip from Russell. But *Aseroe rubra* is what I was after, so I decided to call him again. After some thinking, he remembered that he and Don had found some in Honoka'a, which was fairly close to Hilo. The next morning, I got up in the dark and was out the door at 6:00 a.m. to head north.

The details, as he told me, were: community park, near the parking lot, away from the gymnasium, up a hill, in the grass. So I went to Honoka'a, found the park, the grass, and up the hill I went. As I was just getting to the intended location, I saw a city worker coming toward me on a big riding mower! All I could think was that my only chance to find *Aseroe rubra* had been mowed down just before I arrived.

My only consolation after walking and sniffing around the whole park was that they probably hadn't fruited anyway. But mowed or not, there was nothing to see and photograph. So, I made one more call to Russell, and over my cell phone he guided me to the exact location where he and Don had found them before. However, after several more minutes of circling around (and sniffing, of course), I found nothing.

It was time to get in the car and head back to Hilo, but I refused to give up on what seemed to be a wild goose chase. I walked around one last time in a little wider circle looking in the trees and vegetation surrounding the lawn and then, bingo! There was one single, beautiful, little *Aseroe rubra* with no others (or eggs for that matter) around. I spent the next half hour or so at a photo-mycological feast with the mushroom and a few flies to commune with.

I took every possible still shot and video capture I could think of. Then, as I drove down the road, I savored not only the moment, but also a lifestyle of wild gambles that, most of the time, keep paying off.

Saddle Road, Big Island, Hawaii

Acknowledgements:

I owe a debt of gratitude to my friends and colleagues who have helped me in the creation of this book: to Medea Minnich for her love, patience, and editing. For creative input and advice I thank Marlin Greene, Mike Boom, and Elinoar Shavit (and for her editing help too), and Annette Jarvie for her invaluable proofreading. Special thanks to Dennis Desjardin, and to Tom May, Mike Wood, Peter Buchanan, Richard Robinson and Toshimitsu Fukiharu, for assistance with mushroom identification; Devon Graham, Daniel Winkler, Omon S. Isikhuemhen, Todd Stagnaro, and Jean-Marc Moncalvo for fact verification. Last but not least to Brett Baunton at ArtScan as well as Hal Belmont and the staff at Overseas Printing Corporation for turning this piece of creative work into a book.

Photo credits:

Pg. 10 by Madame Chinchilla; pg. 13 by Tony Young; pg. 21 by Maggie Rogers; pg. 40 by Pedro; pg. 47 Taylor and "young mycologist" by Boonchock Thaitatgoon; pg. 59 Pu'un Ulun and Taylor by Golbart Pitan; pg. 63 upper right by Jacko; pg. 77 upper left and "Partying with Hongo-san" by Akihiro Sawada; pg. 83 center right by Mr. Win; pg. 89 by Tim Geho; pg. 100 upper right by Mike Wood; pg. 101 upper left, by Medea Minnich; pg. 101 upper right and lower right by Elinoar Shavit; pg. 106 Tom and Taylor by Daryl Cox; pg. 125 "Khao Yai" by Boonchock Thaitatgoon, Gary Lincoff by Tom Sargis, "Road food" by Medea Minnich, with Dr. Terry Henkel by Don Bryant, with Dr. Gastón Guzmán by Mark Thomsen, with grade-school class by Medea Minnich, with Tenaya by Medea Minnich, "Hunting desert fungi" by Patrick Lockwood; back cover by Todd Stagnaro; inside jacket photo of Taylor by Patrick Lockwood.

Laetiporus sulphureus, Pennsylvania

Chasing the Rain

Just one last shot . . .

Khao Yai, Thailand

Dr. Rytas Vilgalys with class

Mike Wood of MykoWeb

Road food

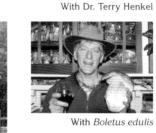
With Dr. Terry Henkel

Gary Lincoff teaching at SOMA camp

With Dr. Gastón Guzmán

Mushroom architecture

With *Boletus edulis*

The oldest umbrella

With Tenaya

Medea & *Aseroe*

Hunting desert fungi

With grade-school class in Caspar, California

Dr. Don Hemmes

Dr. Bruce Ing with Dr. Anne & Zoe Pringle

Elinoar with a "Hen"

Brian Luther at the Puget Sound Mycological Society mushroom fair

PEOPLE, PLACES, AND ORGANIZATIONS

MYCOLOGICAL INDEX